NOW THAT'S A GREAT
QUESTION!

Lauren -
Level Up your leadership
every day

Jeff
Phil 3:12

NOW
THAT'S A
GREAT
QUESTION!

by
JEFF RAKER

Now That's a Great Question! may be purchased for educational, business or sales promotional use. For information please write: Special Markets Department, MoonRaker Enterprises, LLC, ???? Need Your Address ????.

FIRST PAPERBACK EDITION PUBLISHED 2021

Design by Dean Graves

ISBN 978-163877579-9

10 9 8 7 6 5 4 3 2 1

To my wife, Stephanie, who said, "Yes," to the most important question I've ever asked.

To my three children, Kathryn, Caroline, and John who know just how much I love to ask questions.

Table of Contents

Foreword

"I hear you are a Business Coach, I'd like to introduce you to someone".

Summer 2014, Miami, Florida. I'm attending a meeting of swimming officials from around the world and it was at a casual buffet dinner the first evening where I was introduced to Jeff Raker.

Jeff that evening is the same person I've had the immense privilege of getting to know more and more in the years since, positive, curious (full of questions!), a great listener. He is always willing to share and add value from his own expertise and experience once he has asked a few questions to understand the needs of the other.

Years later, on one of our regular video calls, I recall he was struggling a little with writing something to share to his followers and I suggested: "how about video?"

Where did that question come from? Well, as Jeff has evolved and grown in his work, one thing I encouraged him to pay attention to is the idea that: "we are the sum total of all our experiences", so to ask himself what he can do to bring all of that into the service of others.

His experiences? Among his many varied experiences, Jeff was a pastor for decades and so spoke hundreds upon hundreds of times to groups both large and small. From that, it is natural that I've always experienced Jeff most powerfully in person, from his calm yet energising demeanour, to his warm and inviting midwestern baritone voice, to his almost beatific smile. So, "how about video?" was my question.

Foreword

As Jeff explains in parts of this book, he gradually dipped his toes into the water of putting himself out there on video. However, by early 2020, it was wonderful to see that he had found a great niche, creating his series: "The Question for Today", each a short video with a question for us to ponder.

This book captures thirty of Jeff's wonderful questions, and in a carefully designed way to help you take the most possible from each question for yourself.

I know you will take true value from this book and, further, I encourage you to experience Jeff in person when you can, or at least through sight and sound on his videos.

Tom McCallum
February 2021
London, England

Introduction

I had made a mistake and there was nowhere to hide. Filling the role of swimming starter for the World University Games held in Kazan, Russia, I was exposed. Kazan is known as "The gateway to Siberia" and I was a little afraid I would be shown the city gates.

In this beautiful, new, cavernous natatorium, I had hit the start button before I gave instruction to "Take your mark." The international group of athletes on the blocks looked over at me and wondered who was responsible for letting me have the microphone that morning.

After being sternly lectured by my Russian Referee (Evgeny is a really nice guy, and big, and I had messed up his deck), and composing myself, the rest of the starts went off perfectly.

Sitting behind me were two influential men who held the power to decide whether I ever started again on the international stage. We spoke afterwards and one of them asked: "What's the lesson you learned? It's not the mistake that matters but what happens after the mistake. What did you learn?"

I said: "Now that's a great question," and proceeded to share some initial thoughts on the lessons learned.

"Now that's a great question!"

It's the most frequent sentence I hear from my clients over thousands of coaching sessions. There are others:

"I have no idea," in response to a great question.

"That's painful, but good," when we dig to the bottom of "Why?"

Introduction

"I know I'm supposed to ask a question here, but I have no idea what it is!" Now, that's an honest response, and I love it when I hear truth.

How I wish I would have learned the power of asking questions much earlier in my life!

It is the one thing most often highlighted by my clients. They tell me that learning to ask great questions has been the single most important new skill they've acquired. It stands firmly upon the shoulder of the power of self-awareness.

My comfort zone used to be making statements, sharing opinions, and giving unsolicited advice. Now I ask questions. I'm curious. I want to learn so that I know where to start.

Great questions help us in at least these two ways:

First, a great question helps us know what information we need to add to a conversation. Rather than jumping into sharing the information we know, a question helps us start where the other person is. Absent a question, we will start where we are, with what we think the person is asking based on our personal biases toward the words they have spoken.

Second, a great question invites the other person to share more honestly, at a deeper level. After more than three decades of Coaching people, I've come to know that human beings rarely share all that they want to share the first time. They want to know if it's a safe place to go to that place of insight and feeling.

Introduction

In these pages you will be invited to grapple with 30 of my favorite questions. You will meet real clients, including me, who wrestled with these questions that provided light for their next steps. Then you can engage in some personal application projects of varying length, dependent on how deeply you want to dig.

This book is not about sharing information. My goal is transformation of leadership, first of the self, because only then can you effectively lead others.

Questions are powerful. I look forward to hearing your stories about the questions you are asked and that you ask of others.

UESTION 1 | Am I following the Compass or the Calendar today?

he Compass matters more the Calendar. The direction you are heading mat- ?rs more than the speed with which you are getting there.
Jeff Raker

he Purpose Your personal why The Compass sits and beckons you to pay attention. The Calendar comes with a to-do list and deadlines, dangling a reward of satisfaction as you admire the checked boxes of accomplishment. The Compass asks, *"Were these activities taking you in the direction you wanted to go?"*

The Calendar feeds something in each of us. It feels good to see what we have accomplished. But the person who pushes relentlessly ahead is one who will soon find themselves out of physical energy and seeking direction through fogged lenses. The vision will disappear on the treadmill to nowhere.

The only way to live according to the Compass is to engage in a regular rhythm of pause, rest, and reflection. No human being can continue to push without rest. It is more than just sleep. This rhythm helps you step back to see the big picture. Too much activity without rest and reflection makes a leader myopic.

The more you are driven by the Compass, the more you can make choices that get you where you want to go, no matter what is going on around you. Outside forces and other people's choices will put up roadblocks, dig a pit, and create no tres- passing signs. Knowing your compass gives you a steady beacon by which to measure success.

Level Up your Leadership with this Question for Today.

QUESTION 1 | The Story

When things don't go according to plan, it's the Compass that can make the difference. This book is a result of the Covid-19 pandemic. I've had the goal of writing a book since the start of my business. With the onset of the pandemic in 2020, the timing of it moved up. For me, it was a Compass point.

No plan ever completely goes according to plan. A military saying is, *"No plan survives first contact with the enemy."* The next steps become governed by the objective, which is a Compass point.

Mike is a client. His normal job routines blew up in the pandemic. As we walked through next steps, the first step was to clarify his compass. We clarified his why: Why does he exist? What is his purpose in life? This started us down a path to simplifying his focus. The answer became his True North Compass point. Had he started off on the urgent business staring him in the face, he would have missed the most important things that would actually help move things forward. His plans changed due to forces outside of his control. I didn't let him complain. I didn't let him blame. Those are behavioral choices that lead nowhere.

No matter what is happening around Mike, he now knows to allow his Compass to lead the way. Throughout the pandemic, information changed, sometimes daily. Mike could make decisions based on how to move with his personal and business Compass rather than reacting to new news. In some sense, what others decided and did no longer mattered because his Compass remained constant. The calendar shifted. Plans were cancelled and new plans were made based on the same Compass.

QUESTION 1 | The Application

1. Take your calendar and block out Compass time. This is time for reflection, planning, and learning. Consider a 1:1:1 approach: 1 hour per day; 1 day per month; 1 week per year rhythm that some find helpful.

2. Discover your why if you don't know it yet. I would suggest Simon Sinek's *"Find Your Why"* volume or Sherpa Coaching's *"Why It Matters."* (1)

QUESTION 2 | **What am I afraid of?**

In our minds, fears are bigger and scarier than in reality.

The Purpose

Fear is a universal emotion that shows itself in higher blood pressure, increased heart rate, butterflies in the gut, and a flushed face. All leaders are afraid. Knowing what you are afraid of builds an essential step for leveling up your leadership.

Fear gains power from secrecy. Unnamed fear will wreak havoc with your mind and emotions. Name it, expose it, give room to it, and you can lead through it. This is leadership. Successful leaders don't allow fear to be in the lead. Leveling up your leadership is about leading yourself despite the fear, through the anxiety, using the pressure instead of allowing your actions to be determined by it. If you seek to fight against the fear, telling yourself not to be afraid or to stop feeling anxious, you will lose every time. Own it. Admit it. Expose it – and then you can move past it.

The most basic fear is what we think other people believe about us. Fear of failure is real. Most of the time it's not actually the failure that is the issue. Ask yourself what the failure would mean to you, *What would it say about you?* This will help peel back the layers to uncover the root fear.

Sometimes fears are real. Most of the time fears are in our minds. In our minds, those fears are bigger and scarier than in reality.

Ask yourself this question, expose your fear, and then lead yourself through it.

Level Up your Leadership with this Question for Today.

QUESTION 2 | The Story

I have been afraid more times than I have fingers and toes. When a staff member needed to find a new position at a different place, the dreaded conversation, I felt fear. Standing on a block for the start of a race at the Junior National swimming championships, fear was with me. Fear tried to box me in when I started shooting the *"1-Minute Question for Today"* videos, the genesis of this book. Fear drove me to be reserved and not myself, focusing on what I thought others might think about me, rather than about the message I could bring.

Fear comes up when I'm speaking with an Athletic Director or an HR manager, pitching them my coaching business.

It's the fear of what failure means to me that is the problem. Will it mean I am a failure? Will it mean others see me as a failure? This is fuel for fear. I realized my fears were based on my assumptions of what I thought others might think.

None of us has the superpower to read other people's minds, and yet that is exactly what use to make we base our fearful choices.

35 years after my last swimming competition in college, I was competing at Masters Nationals in the 200 freestyle. Three-quarters of the way through the race fear crept alongside me. I couldn't see where anyone else was in the pool. Fear said, "You'll be last and embarrassed." Suddenly my final turn was upon me and it was terrible. The worst turn in history because I was focused on my fears and not what I was doing. This is how fear operates. Rather than lead myself, I allowed fear to lead. In the end my fears were scarier than the reality. I had won a National Championship.

The fear I felt was hollow. I allowed fear to be the leader rather than leading myself.

QUESTION 2 | The Application

1. Remember a time when you operated out of fear. What did you stop doing or pursuing? What did you do instead? Go to the level of emotions as well as thoughts and actions.

2. Make a list of the kinds of fears you have, i.e., spiders, heights, public speaking. What do you do when you come face to face with such situations? What do you not do because of your fears?

3. Choose one of your fears. Make a list of the things you do and don't control that are associated with your fear. This will help you move forward with tangible results as you focus on what you can control.

QUESTION 3 | What can I learn from this?

Failure is never final, but it is a wonderful teacher to an attentive student.

The Purpose   Leaders are learners. *What can I learn from this?* is a constant companion question of a successful leader. Stop learning and you stop leading. Create a learning environment that isn't afraid to ask this hard question. It's not about finding blame. It is about uncovering the systems, processes, assumptions, and methods that are and are not working.

Failure is never final, but it is a wonderful teacher to an attentive student. Some of the best leadership lessons you learn come from failures. There are three ways to fail: quit, don't try, and don't learn anything.

Imbed this question in the fabric of your day, for successes and failures. Ask yourself the lessons learned each day. Ask this when a project is successfully delivered to a client. Ask your team, *What can we learn from this?* When you run into an unanticipated roadblock and it takes time to find your way through, use this question to grow.

It is accurately said, if you are not succeeding at what you pursue, then you are not failing often enough. In failure you learn what won't work and gain wisdom about how to make something work. You can also learn when it's time to cut bait and move on to what's next.

In response to a question about his missteps, Thomas Edison once said, *"I have not failed 10,000 times—I've successfully found 10,000 ways that will not work."*

Level Up your Leadership with this Question for Today.

QUESTION 3 | The Story

One way I give back to sports is volunteering my time as a swim official. For a short time I had the privilege of being a FINA (the international governing body for aquatic sports) starter for the United States, meaning the four of us on the list could represent the U.S. internationally. I was coached by a mentor, Pat Lunsford, and, early on, his question was posed in a different way: *"Every start has a lesson. Learn the lesson. Forget the start."*

While in Kazan, Russia, known as the Gateway to Siberia, standing in a beautiful, new, cavernous natatorium, on one heat I pushed the start button before I invited the athletes to, *"Take your mark."* I wondered if I'd be shown the gates of the city. But the next five starts went perfectly. The lesson: it's not the mistake that defines you but what you do after the mistake.

In Irvine, CA., at a swim meet ranked just below our U.S. Olympic Trials, I listened to an older, more experienced starter's thoughts and made a shift in where I was standing on deck. This choice led to some shaky starts. I learned a lesson: *Do what you know how to do.*

What can I learn from this? is the opposite of *Failure is final.*

It's not a failure that defines you but rather your willingness to learn. It's not the terrible start that matters as much as the next start. A leader wants to know from her people, *What did you learn from this?* You don't want to ask, *Why did this happen?* because it will lead to defensiveness rather than learning. What can you learn from this? will grow your people and you will get to the why did this happen? part that you want.

Examine your behaviors, your successes and your failures, for lessons. The people who succeed the most are the ones who fail the most – if along the way they look for the lessons.

QUESTION 3 | The Application

1. Consider a recent failure or mistake. What went wrong and, more importantly, ask yourself, When did it go wrong? Examine it. Look underneath the fact that it just didn't work. Find out why.

2. Do you personalize failure? In other words, when you fail, do you translate that into an internal feeling of, I'm a failure? Consider doing some reading from Dr. Martin Seligman and his "*3 P's - Personal - Pervasive - Permanent.*" It can help you understand why some of your failures can be so devastating. (2)

3. What does it mean to fail forward? What are some practical steps you can take to do this in your life?

QUESTION 4 | **Where do I get in my own way?**

Self-awareness is the foundation of self-leadership.

The Purpose Not everything we do is helpful. How many times have you said, I really need to stop doing that? Successful leaders realize they have blind spots. This isn't a question about focusing in on your weaknesses. It's a self-awareness question.

Self-awareness is the foundation of self-leadership. You have to be aware of what doesn't work. Ask your people. Ask your spouse or trusted friend.

Do you share too much? Do you talk about others behind their backs? Is your default response anger? Are you accusatory or condescending? If your people experience you this way then it's a problem whether you think it is or not. If you are married, ask your spouse. Ask this question of a significant other, your boss, and your subordinates. Ask and then listen. How well do you observe yourself. How well do you receive feedback, helping you see yourself more clearly?

Choose not to travel the pathway of defensiveness. Bathe such a conversation in curiosity. Let this question – and the responses – lead to more questions, such as:

- Where does that happen?
- Can you give me a specific example?
- What would be a different approach you would recommend?

Level Up your Leadership with this Question for Today.

QUESTION 4 | The Story

Early in my thirties I began to invite feedback into my life. Seeing the benefits of it, I only wish I'd done it earlier and more often.

I started a practice of inviting a trusted friend to breakfast or coffee, prompting them with some questions that were not rhetorical. I wanted honest feedback.

First: What are the three adjectives that come to mind when you think of me?

Second: What is one thing I should stop doing?

Third: What is one thing I should start doing?

Then I would listen. I would ask for specifics and details. Sometimes I would say, *"Really?"* And my trusted friend would laugh with a sly, *"Oh, yes!"* It can be a painful conversation but so very good.

In 2008, I added another layer to this feedback via some self-assessment questions. I borrowed some of them from Michael Hyatt (3) on his blog. I also added some of my own. Questions included:

- What accomplishments am I most proud of from the past year?
- What did I not do that I wish I would have done?
- What rhythms did I follow and how will I take some forward into the new year?
- What physical, mental, emotional, and spiritual goals do have for next year?

These have been helpful disciplines, because I know I can get off course far too easily without realizing it.

QUESTION 4 | The Application

1. Be honest with yourself: Where do I get in my own way? Consider relationships that aren't working. Think about the last time you got defensive and argumentative. Could you have approached those circumstances differently?

2. Self-assess your ability to hear, receive, and respond to feedback. Are you open to it or defensive about it? How can you be more open to feedback?

3. Make a list of questions for self-assessment. Fill them out right away and then put them in your calendar when you will answer them each year or each quarter. Pick a rhythm that works for the way you work.

Email me at Jeff@levelupleadershipcoach.com if you'd like a copy of the questions I use to evaluate the past year and propel myself forward to the next.

QUESTION 5 | What do I control?

You control YOU and almost nothing else.

The Purpose A person's greatest anxieties and frustrations often come from trying to control what they do not control. This question has a companion one: What do I not control? By answering one, you answer the other.

Control is an illusion most of the time. In my lifetime I have experienced the Iran hostage crisis, the 9/11 terrorist attacks, SARS, and then Covid-19. Each of these had its own way of telling me that I was not in control of as much as I thought I was.

When you are not in control, what happens to you? What are you afraid of? How do you react? Controlling people usually becomes loud, bossy, and demanding. Is this you?

Seeking to control things that are out of your control is one of the main sources of anxiety, pressure, and fear in your life. Having been married for 35 years so far, I know I cannot change my wife. She cannot change me. If we try to live there it will lead to frustration and perhaps end the marriage.

At its most basic level, you control YOU. You don't control other people. You don't control most events around your life. Level up your leadership by deciding what you do and what you don't control.

Level up your leadership by discerning what you do and what you don't control.

QUESTION 5 | The Story

A client was, and is, far smarter than I am. But Stuart did something that was a stupid time waster, causing him to lose sleep, and therefore not be at his best. This Ph.D. in the medical field would spend hours (I'm talking three and four hours) before a meeting writing out every possible scenario and direction for that meeting. If the person Stuart was meeting with, usually an M.D., said this, then he would say that. On and on he went, considering every possible tangent, no matter how small.

Stuart arrived at a coaching session with a smirk on his face. I knew there had been a breakthrough. I was excited to hear the story behind it. Two days earlier he had been scheduled for a meeting at 1 p.m., and found himself at 9 a.m. writing out his scenarios. At 9:30 the M.D. opened Stuart's door and said an appointment had cancelled, so why not meet now. Stuart found himself flushed but not saying no.

"So how did the meeting go?" I asked.

"It went really well. I knew every answer to his questions."

I laughed aloud. He soon joined me.

Stuart was seeking to control everything around him, fearful that he didn't know enough, or couldn't go in cold. He learned that he did control his emotions and his ability to pause and think before responding. He did not control the other person, no matter how much he tried.

The company just gained hours of Stuart's time. Stuart gained hours in his day, able to spend more time with his family and on his own self-care. All of this because he found he could let go of seeking to control people and the circumstances around him.

QUESTION 5 | The Application

1. Do you consider yourself a controlling person? What do others say? Write down a few characteristics of a controlling person. Does this describe you?

2. Consider what would be the opposite of control for you? It's not reckless or out-of-control, but more along the lines of chill or relaxed. Use your word as an acronym, listing out the behaviors of a chill or relaxed (or your word) person. Begin to find ways to incorporate these behaviors into your actions and the words into your verbal communication.

QUESTION 6 | What are my core values?

Values are the hills on which you will choose to die.

The Purpose Understanding your core values will help you understand other people. Core values act like filters through which we see circumstances and hear words. You also may have some core values that you express in words but you aren't living out with your actions.

As you lead others, as you coach up their leadership, your values will be your guide. Your core values lead directly to your behaviors. Values are the hills on which you will choose to die. They are the guardrails that hem in behavior. If a core value for you is honesty, then when you have a chance to lie to seal a deal, you will always choose to tell the truth instead.

The same goes for the team, division, or group that you lead. What are the core values of your team? If your team isn't on the same page, start with the values that will then shape the behaviors necessary for success. Have everyone share their personal core values first. Spend the time getting to know the personal hills that make up the team. Knowing the personal core values of everyone on your team will build a foundation on which to grow cohesion for the values of the team.

Discover and commit to your core values. Are you ordering your life around them? If not, they are not really your core values.

Level Up your Leadership with this Question for Today.

QUESTION 6 | The Story

As we walked through a core values exercise together, a client realized he was not living out what he said he held high. He had identified the value of financial freedom but wasn't following through. He was working hard, he thought, to provide for his family. What he realized was his long days and working after the kids went to bed was really about wanting more things. The pursuit of wanting more things had created a situation where debt was eating up the paychecks before they arrived. It was not financial freedom but rather the opposite: financial prison.

I asked, *"What would you be doing if you experienced true financial freedom?"*

Our conversation and the realizations that followed led to changes in his behavior. I asked him to settle on his core values and then list one or two (at most) key behaviors that would lead to living out each value. Two people with financial freedom as a value might have two different primary behaviors to pursue.

Specifically with this client, he sat down with his wife and together they laid out a path to true financial freedom. What would they do if they were financially free? What did it mean to them? They had to define it first and then decide on a plan to live it out. Together, they reduced debt, first by stopping new purchases. He shifted his schedule, and had the flexibility to do that, so they could spend more time as a whole family. They expressed their fears about this shift and wrote out the places of greatest temptation they thought they would face: fancy coffee rather than making it at home came at the top of the list. Not much each time, but compounded, it was a lot of money.

Now, they spend money on themselves, creating memories and developing curiosity in their children.

What are your core values and are you living them out?

QUESTION 6 | The Application

1. Write out your top 5 core values and define each of them with a couple of sentences.

2. For each value, list two to three behaviors that you can do to live out that value in everyday life and work.

3. Share these with a friend for some honest feedback, because accountability is helpful. If you're using this book in a group or with your leadership team, use a meeting to go through these. It's worth the time and effort.

UESTION 7 | What would that look like?

ractice what you want and your vision will get closer every day.

he Purpose This is such a great question to get you unstuck and moving forward. Being a leader means doing more than just dreaming, although dreaming is an essential component. This question helps you get specific. Only then can you walk the steps to making the dream a reality.

If you were a drone, flying at 10,000 feet above your life, what would you see yourself doing?

What would it look like if you reached your goal? Be specific. What feelings would you feel? Where would it take you? What else would come along with the accomplishment?

Where do you have a difficult or intractable relationship? Apply this question: *What would the relationship look like if it were healthier?* As you identify the behaviors, begin practicing them.

When you know what would be happening, it gives you a foothold to begin living into the desired reality.

Ask yourself this question about the most important relationship in your life. If you want better communication, what would it look like? If you desire greater intimacy, what would that look like?

Level Up your Leadership with this Question for Today.

QUESTION 7 | The Story

Lisa was working her way toward a job she was passionate about, out of an independent contractor job that, while it paid the bills, was not fulfilling. We asked this question: *"What would it look like if you were in that job?"* She was creating this job from scratch.

This was a real, tangible conversation, because Lisa knew the job she wanted full-time. She was already beginning to establish it as a side gig. We began by listing out the behaviors she would do in that job. Where would she spend her time? What would she be doing? What would be the priorities? What keystone habits would leverage her greatest strengths? What weaknesses would she need to guard against?

This was arduous work, as coaching is. Lisa had to be honest with herself about her fears, the things that kept her in her comfort zone. Once she owned them, she could see a clear path through them. Still hard, but a way forward.

We compared her vision of then to what she was doing now, identifying similarities and differences. This work gave Lisa a framework to live into, moving from her comfort zone, through the fear zone, and into the learning and growth zones. The steps were purposeful now, like laying out a pathway through a garden, she knew how to get to the other side.

The smallest actionable step can move you in the right direction. Today, Lisa is living into that passionate job, rather than stuck in her unfulfilling comfort zone.

QUESTION 7 | The Application

1. Consider a goal or dream that you have yet to accomplish. Ask yourself this question and begin writing down the answers. And keep asking the question until you dig down to a doable thing.

2. Name the fears that are creating barriers and hurdles for you.

3. Build this question into your normal routine with your direct reports and your boss. When expectations are given by you or to you, this question will help in clarifying the expectation.

QUESTION 8 | Am I making this personal?

Making it all about you will mess things up.

The Purpose When we take things personally, we mess things up. When you react emotionally, or with too much emotion for the stimulus of the words or circumstances, ask yourself this question.

Someone's angry with you and you get sucked into that vortex of emotion and think it's about you. It never is. Another person's anger is always about them. Don't make it personal. Ask these questions instead: "What's up?" or "What's that about?"

Defensiveness is your first clue that you're making it about you. If you immediately seek to disagree or argue with the other person, you might have taken it personally. Making something personal indicates you feel threatened. Maybe you are trying to project a certain image of yourself, and when words or circumstances shift that desired perception, you make it personal and act out.

Suddenly your actions have nothing to do with the issue or theme at hand. It has everything to do with you instead.

Consider your relationship with accountability. Most often, leaders avoid holding their people accountable because they don't like conflict. You just made it all about you, rather than the issue. This is a subtle leadership trap, always lurking at the edges ready to pounce.

Level Up your Leadership with this Question for Today.

QUESTION 8 | The Application

Anger: it's always about you.
Defensiveness: it's always about you.
Fear of not wanting to confront someone: it's always about you.

When you assume others will be upset with you or not like you, should you decide on this or that course of action? It's all about you.

Making things personal happens all the time. In order to lead yourself, it is vital that you become aware of when this happens to you.

I sometimes think, "If I'd only become aware of this issue earlier in my life, I would have been a more effective leader." I noticed it mostly when I received feedback, the constructive kind. I loved hearing about what was going well. I disliked intensely when told what was not going well and what others said needed to be fixed. I made it all about me.

I clearly remember sitting in a conference room receiving feedback from two board members. Some of it was tough, although it was intended to be constructive. I sat back in my chair and became silent. I crossed my arms. I look back at myself and think, *"What arrogance!"*

I thought it was all about me and not the issues of effectiveness and teamwork. The goal of the Church meant nothing, at least that's what my response communicated. I effectively detached from leading the team, to resisting change in myself. I didn't know at the time that leadership is all about the person of the leader. It's not personal. It is about the leader becoming a better leader by getting out of their own way.

What's your story about making things personal and how it gets in your way?

QUESTION 8 | The Application

1. How do you react when someone brings an accusation or suggests poor behavior on your part? What about during a performance review?

2. What does your response to feedback communicate to others?

3. Do an Internet search of "quit taking it personally," to see images and quotes that will help seat this boundary firmly in your heart.

QUESTION 9 | How can I pause?

A pause may be the most powerful leadership tool you have.

The Purpose The importance of the pause in leadership cannot be overstated. Coach yourself with this question to prepare ahead of time for both expected and unexpected circumstances that may bring an emotional reaction from you.

Some leaders speak quickly into each and every circumstance and conversation. A pause would help. Some leaders process out loud rather than thinking before they speak. A pause would assist them. A long pause, called silence, is helpful. How are you with silence?

If a relationship is conflicted and you are going to see that person prepare ahead of time for how you will take a pause before speaking. A deep breath works well, although, if done overtly, it can communicate negatively to the other person. So, be careful with your body language.

Taking a moment to think before speaking will demonstrate the seriousness with which you are communicating. You will end up speaking fewer words, and that's always better. More words will more quickly mess things up.

What keeps you from pausing? Everyone is different in what drives them. How are you with silence? Silence is a powerful leadership tool. But you can't use it if you don't learn to pause.

Level Up your Leadership with this Question for Today.

QUESTION 9 | The Story

One of my favorite clients, probably because we are so much alike, needed to speak into every conversation. He could not sit quietly and ask questions at first. He was a fixer whose first instinct was to speak up, processing his thoughts out loud. He would stir up a verbal contest just so he could fix it.

Once he realized this, and accepted it – which are two distinct steps – we were able to create a pathway to a different behavior. He realized that his mind left the room, literally going to all the possible bad things that could happen if his staff didn't make a correct decision. He worried about his job and then his family. His comfort zone was fixing and he loved to be involved, mostly because he connected it to protecting his family.

His desire was noble. But the behaviors that emanated from his desire were not helpful. Some people on his staff pushed back, energized by getting into the fray. Others sat back, because they did not enjoy conflict at all. In the end, everyone left the room feeling like they had accomplished little.

He experimented with a couple of different actions to help him pause. It was a process of finding the right thing that not only worked for him but also didn't communicate negatively through body language. When he sat up straight in his chair, it communicated he was struggling and ready for the fight. It helped him pause, but it wasn't helpful to his team. Eventually he worked with his feet, under the table. Simply moving them around, back and forth, he felt the friction and it fixed his mind in the present moment. He was able to pause.

He still enjoys entering the fray and fixing things. He's learned that when he overplays it, he gets in trouble. What about you?

QUESTION 9 | The Application

1. Spend some time concentrating on your breathing. Just breathe deeply and slowly. What's the purpose? The one who controls their breathing will control their brain. This will help you pause.

2. Take a day or a week to record personal observations of yourself. How often do you NOT pause? Then get curious about what is happening. The people who are best at diets keep a food journal so that they know exactly what they are doing, rather than guessing. The same with leadership. Find out what you actually do. Then you can do something about it.

3. When you encounter a conversation, and you want to speak, experiment with one of two things: if you are standing, balance on the balls of your feet for five seconds. If you are seated, press your feet into the floor for five seconds. Both actions will help keep you present and able to pause.

QUESTION 10 | What would I do differently next time?

Leaders think in terms of behaviors. Not everything in a failed venture is bad or negative.

The Purpose One of my all-time favorite questions! Successful leaders don't beat themselves up over a failure or mistake. They learn. This question will help. It's also an excellent question to ask a direct report or colleague when something didn't work – or even if it was a success.

Unsuccessful leaders beat themselves up over lost opportunities or failed initiatives: *"You're so stupid! You can't do anything right!"* These are not leadership thoughts.

A successful leader takes their bumps and bruises, then learns the lessons: What would I do differently next time? This question moves a leader forward, rather than remaining mired in the past. Failure is found all along the path to success. Some of a leader's greatest lessons are learned in their failures.

Leaders think in terms of behaviors. Not everything in a failed venture is bad or negative. Maybe you would begin differently next time. Perhaps you would say you could have persevered. Did you move too quickly or too slowly? Did you have the right people around you? These are all lessons for the next time.

Make the first question about what worked. Then you will see more clearly what didn't work. Start with the positive, then you will know what you would have done differently.

Leaders are learners and one of the best teachers is failure. Reframing failure with this forward-looking question creates greater ownership.

QUESTION 10 | The Story

Business leaders and athletes have more in common than differences. First and foremost, they are people. Every human being is wired in similar ways. For an elite athlete, failure has to be a stepping stone to learning. The same is true in business.

Whether my client is an athlete or a business leader, a key theme along our journey always includes how they deal with failure. I like to use the word experiments. Because not all experiments work, using experiments helps us reframe what we're attempting to do to make everything work.

A sports coach client was used to telling an athlete what they did and didn't do following a race. I encouraged him to try an experiment with asking a question. It was out of his comfort zone and it worked. He quickly saw his athletes taking ownership of their choices in a race. When the athletes didn't have an answer to "What would you do differently next time?" the question challenged them to be more aware.

The next experiment for this Coach came in the order of his words. *"Ask what went well, before you allow an athlete, or yourself, to get to what could be improved."* Once again, it worked. By stretching his comfort zone, and doing what he asked his athletes to do (trust your Coach) he found new life for both himself and his team.

A business client experimented with only asking questions, as she was prone to making statements. She found a result similar to the sports coach. Her people began coming up with their own answers, owning their behaviors and choices. She was coaching rather than managing and it was freeing.

Where can this question come into play in your life and in coaching those you lead?

QUESTION 10 | The Application

1. Where would you self-assess your approach to failure? On a 1-10 scale, are you a 1 who is completely devastated by failure or a 10 who always uses failures to learn helpful lessons?

2. What would you change that would help you grow from a 6 to a 7? Or from a 4 to a 5? Be specific about a behavior.

3. Consider a recent failure. Was it in a conversation when you said something that wasn't helpful? Was it a project that didn't turn out as planned? What would you do differently next time?

_____
_____
_____
_____
_____
_____
_____
_____
_____
_____
_____
_____
_____
_____
_____
_____
_____
_____
_____
_____
_____
_____
_____
_____
_____
_____
_____
_____
_____
_____
_____
_____

QUESTION 11 | How do I talk to myself?

"If you think you can, you can. If you think you can't, you're right."
- Henry Ford

The Purpose   Self-talk is one of the more powerful leadership behaviors in your toolbox. You may miss some of what others say, but you hear everything you say to yourself. This is both helpful and not so helpful. In a very real sense, your words create the pathway you walk in life.

Your brain processes about 60,000 thoughts per day, most of them unconsciously. And, for some reason, your brain loves to gravitate to the negative, ruminating on what didn't go well, what needs to change, and what wasn't perfect.

What are the words you say to yourself? Are they encouraging? Are they demeaning? In reality, most people speak to themselves in a way they would never allow their friends to do. Friends would get punched. Your words about yourself create internal bruises. Those words can limit your energy and motivation – or they can increase it.

Use this question to begin to believe in yourself. When you hear words that aren't encouraging, wonder aloud how you could change them. Be careful here. You might have a tendency to beat yourself up for failing to encourage yourself. It's a weird cycle. I call it curiosity without condemnation. Just be curious about where the words came from, then about how you could change those words.

Level Up your Leadership with this Question for Today.

QUESTION 11 | The Story

You may not hear every word that others say to you, but I guarantee you hear every word you say to yourself.

Self-talk is a consistent clue to me about where some of my work goes with a client. We are so very mean to ourselves. Our words will either build us up, or tear us down; they will either motivate us forward or tie us to the past, preventing us from reaching our goals.

A group of swim officials was standing on deck during a break in a national level meet held in Greensboro, N.C. Someone asked what I was doing these days for work, having heard I made a shift. After describing what an Executive Leadership Coach does, she asked, *"So, what's your word of wisdom for today?"*

I reminded the group of the swim official's motto: *"The swimmer always gets the benefit of the doubt."* This means that if I think I saw an infraction, I didn't. If I don't raise my hand immediately upon seeing a potential disqualification, then I can't call it. If I'm pretty sure I know what an athlete is doing underwater, the evidence lending itself to an illegal kick or pull, but I can't see the kick or pull, then there is nothing to call.

They nodded in agreement.

I continued, *"What if we gave the benefit of the doubt to those around us, and also to ourselves? What difference would that make in our lives?"*

Heads shook in agreement. *"That is so good,"* one person said.

Take a look at the application questions and suggestions for ways to implement this in your life and to encourage others.

QUESTION 11 | The Application

1. Keep a running journal today of how many times you say to yourself, should have, ought to, and have to. You may be amazed. These are words that beat you down.

2. Begin to shift your self-talk from those three phrases to I could have or I can. These are words that create ownership of your actions in the past and encouragement for what's next.

3. When you notice negative self-talk, become curious about what led to it: I wonder what that's about? Rather than, You are so stupid, you can't even do this right! Take the gentle approach on yourself and you will find greater motivation and deeper resilience as a leader.

QUESTION 12 | What will my tombstone read if I continue to lead the way I do today?

Is the path you are traveling the path you really want in the end?

The Purpose Eternity questions are sometimes the perfect theme to bring perspective. If I died today, what would people say about me as a leader? What would be the words on my tombstone?

Leaders who become myopic as they focus on temporary things, such as money or titles, will sacrifice long-term stability and effectiveness. These leaders may find themselves alone, with no one to celebrate the successes. One image to remember may be the Tortoise and the Hare fable. Successful leaders certainly take risks. But satisfying success brings others along for the ride. Sometimes it's a long, slow ride.

Reconsider Question 1: *Am I following the Compass or the Calendar today?* It's the compass that helps a leader live out their most deeply held values and beliefs.

This tombstone question can be shocking to the system, but sometimes that's what a leader needs. Is the path you are traveling the path you really want in the end?

What would your tombstone say right now about your leadership approach and what do you want it to say? If those are different answers, then what needs to shift?

Level Up your Leadership with this Question for Today.

QUESTION 12 | The Story

Most often when I pose this question, the response is thoughtful silence. I think that's appropriate. A few words may come to mind after a time: kind, helpful, generous…then it becomes a homework project. Really think on this one. The shock comes when today's leadership words are different from tombstone leadership words.

The shock is most often the result of short-term focus or even shortcuts that violated personal values.

Take Abby for instance. Abby confronted this question and dove deep. What she found was not what she wanted others to say about her. Words like *"short tempered," "demanding,"* or *"micro-manager"* came up. She wouldn't have minded *"driven"* or one who had *"high expectations"* for her people.

We made a list of what was now and what she'd like it to be. Along the journey, Abby discovered new ways of relating to her people and new behaviors that helped her stay on the path she desired. She admitted to feeling fearful: "What if my team doesn't do what they need to because I'm not pushing them like before?" She called me a few months after our sessions ended to report, with great joy, that her people were doing great. The team was more effective and productive.

Abby said, *"I feel more fulfilled and less anxious. Even my family has noticed the difference. Thank you."*

QUESTION 12 | The Application

1. Write out three or four words that you believe describe your leadership today. Make them descriptive words. I would encourage you to ask some people for their honest response to make sure you have an accurate assessment.

2. What words do you want to be there that are not there at present?

3. Now think in terms of behaviors. What behaviors will lead to the descriptive words you want? For the words you want to keep, what behaviors help you grow in that theme? Settle on one or two behaviors for each word. Be specific. What would you actually do?

QUESTION 13 | What am I angry about?

Anger is always about the person who is angry.

The Purpose   Anger will rarely, if ever, get a leader where they want to go. Anger personalizes a situation, distracting efforts from solving the real issue at hand. I tell clients to always remember that a person's anger is always about the person, not anyone else. What does your anger tell you about you?

The source of anger is situational – an emotional response to a trigger. Often anger is an attempt to avoid or deflect, such as when a person gets defensive. I find with clients that when they push back quickly, and forcefully, with their words, that I've gotten very close to a sensitive topic, or perhaps pain, in their life.

Level Up Leadership is about being able to step out of the situation and observe yourself. The leader who is able to do this will lead with rational thought rather than emotional recklessness.

In answering this question, focus on the issues and circumstances rather than the people. It may be the actions of a person that set off your anger, but it's not the person. It's the behavior. What is it that the person did? Perhaps that action violated a personal or company value. This would lead to a feeling of anger. Make sure you know what the issue is. It's not about the person, it's about you.

Anger is a choice. No one has the power to make us angry.

Level Up your Leadership with this Question for Today.

QUESTION 13 | The Story

"Anger is my comfort zone," Kris concluded. He was right. Whether it was being unsure of what to do next, or frustration because someone didn't do what was asked, he reverted to anger more often than other responses. *"And what is that about?"* I would consistently ask.

Kris realized he got angry when his people stopped short of their potential or at least his desire for their potential. One trigger we uncovered occurred when a team member didn't fulfill a delegated task. Kris made it all about himself. Kris was concerned how this failure would make Kris look to others.

After asking some questions, he discovered a habit of not explaining tasks as clearly as possible. He left blanks for his people to fill in by themselves, which never ends well.

On the DISC assessment (3), Kris is a High D, one of the highest I've encountered. The tendency here can be to leave words out, as if everyone would or should understand: how can someone not understand?

As Kris owned his tendencies and recognized his comfort zone default response, he developed a new response: C.H.I.L.L. This is the new behavior he wanted to use for his response in situations that would previously have led to anger. He identified a behavior for each letter and created change that resulted in better communication and higher performance for his people. As he became clear with himself and the behaviors he wanted, it helped him be clear to his people as he laid out expectations.

QUESTION 13 | The Application

1. Take a few moments to write out the scenario of a recent angry response. What happened? What were some possible triggers? Explore. Be curious.

2. What would be the opposite of anger for you? Rather than an angry response you would like to choose _____.
Use that word as an acronym and identify a behavior for each letter. This will give you a positive place to focus when you encounter triggers that normally would turn you to anger.

For instance: C.A.L.M.

Clear my lungs with a deep breath and full exhale
Attend to my location: press my feet into the floor, see the colors and shapes around me
Lean toward the other person to help me listen, before speaking, if I choose to speak at all
Make a positive statement first

QUESTION 14 | Do I like myself?

Own who you are after you discover who you are.

The Purpose Just as a growing leader tends to have a growing team, the leader who likes herself has a positive team that encourages one another. It all starts with the leader.

The second level of the Level Up Leadership Coaching process is *"Self-Compassion."* The acknowledgment of strengths and weaknesses, of successes and past failures, is an essential first step. It gives a clear and honest picture of yourself. Then accept it. Own it. *Self-Compassion* is realizing who you are and being okay with it. It's okay to not be completely okay. It's also okay to change. This is a crucial step in leading well. If a leader is consistently seeking to push aside what is true, they will lose every time. It will lead to a path strewn with boulders of frustration, depression, anger, and more.

Leaders who like themselves will have a self-talk that is positive. That self-talk will come out in how the leader talks to her people. If a leader does not like herself, she will tend to point out all the negative things of others. Compassion to yourself leads to compassion to and for others. Compassion is far more powerful than confidence.

Own who you are after you discover who you are. There are always things we are good at. There are always ways to improve. Liking yourself is about owning an honest assessment of both sides of this leadership coin. Arrogance is believing you are better than you really are.

Level Up your Leadership with this Question for Today.

QUESTION 14 | The Story

Her comfort zone was being mean to herself. She was astonished and embarrassed at the realization. She knew how to be negative and tell herself she wasn't good enough. If she changed to accepting herself, it would be foreign territory.

Refusing to accept herself was keeping her in a negative state of mind. Truth is something I deal with in coaching, often with the firm phrase: *"Is that really true?"*

The most impactful message may have been, *"You are valuable and deserve more worthy words."* Many people don't believe this. She didn't. Part of that was because of her familiarity with this behavior. The other was she didn't believe she was worthwhile enough for more positive words. As I walked alongside her in this journey of Coaching, her relationship with herself became the key to unlocking a more positive and hope-filled future. The pitfall of not liking herself infected everything:

- Lack of honesty in communication meant her people were confused rather than working in a truthful environment
- She assumed conflict would happen and would change course without any real evidence
- Anger or emotional outbursts would happen because she wasn't grounded in truth but was trying to push it away

Liking yourself isn't selfish. My client blossomed as she accepted her good points and her growth points. This change brought new insights in how she saw other people, removing the filters that had obscured the wealth of good and positive surrounding her life. Her people were more engaged, had more energy, and were being more creative – no longer wondering who they would get when they approached their leader, my client, with a new idea.

QUESTION 14 | The Application

1. What do you seek to keep at arms' length, refusing to accept that this is really the way you are? Perhaps asking a few close-trusted friends will help bring clarity here.

2. If these things you push aside are true, what does that mean to you? About you? Dig here a little bit. For instance, a basic human fear is often named as *"fear of failure,"* but, more often than not, the real fear underneath is *"what will other people think of me if I fail?"*

3. Consider a leadership motto for yourself, one that is accepting of who you are, while infusing hope in growth. *"I am flawed and I'm growing every day." "I don't know it all like I'd like to, but I will learn something new today."*

QUESTION 15 | Are you the same in public as in private? Private as in public?

The consistent leader is the successful leader.

The Purpose Integrity is defined by consistency, when the private life of a leader matches the public life of that leader, and vice versa. You need not look very far, nor watch too many newscasts, to realize that private and public are merging in our digital world.

Are you the same in public as you are in private? The same in private as you are in public?

Consistency of character is crucial to successful leadership. Eventually, what you do in private will be shouted from the rooftop. It's just the way life works. What behaviors and choices in your private life would you like to keep hidden from others? Your honest assessment will light the pathway of change.

Do you have integrity between your private life and your public life? When people experience you in public, can they have confidence it's the same they would experience in private? When people experience you in private, are they confident it will be the same when they're in public? The impact of integrity, a fully integrated you, cannot be understated. When there are no surprises, people are more at ease – as well as more motivated.

Level Up your Leadership with this Question for Today.

QUESTION 15 | The Story

Most stories in this category have a tragic ending. There is illegal activity that is uncovered. There are words spoken into a hot mic and a broadcaster loses his job. There are pictures posted from the past and it ends a career.

I've never become aware of a client's hidden behavior, but that doesn't mean it wasn't there. I've known plenty of people who practiced destructive habits in private that eventually derailed careers and relationships. Everyone does stupid things sometimes. It doesn't mean they can never win again.

Let me share highlights about one tragic choice that didn't end in tragedy but rather in triumph. A Pastor confesses an affair to his wife. Her first response, after throwing up, is to ask him to leave, but not permanently. They lost jobs, lost housing, and burned through savings. After counseling, and keeping their commitment to the marriage, the couple stayed together. She demonstrated the forgiveness they had always taught and believed.

Today, they have a marriage ministry, traveling the country inspiring couples to higher and stronger commitments to their vows. The scars of past failures are the very thing that can become life-giving to others, if we're willing to share. It takes courage to be vulnerable.

Be assured, your private activities will come to light. If they have already, don't let it be the final word. Use the scars, and the pain, and the lessons, to add value to the lives of others. If you recognize some behaviors you would be embarrassed for others to discover, today is a great day to begin to change.

QUESTION 15 | The Application

1. Choose one action that is inconsistent in your life. Just one. Understand what leads you to that behavior. Keep a journal of when it happens. What are the triggers?

2. Write out two alternatives to that behavior. For instance, if you find yourself slipping into this behavior at 10 p.m., when you are alone, choose to connect with someone at 9:30 p.m. In other words, divert yourself.

3. Take it easy on yourself. Everyone has things they'd like to change or need to change. Pay attention to your self-talk, shifting it to encouraging and positive words.

QUESTION 16 | What happened?

Curiosity is oxygen to the leader looking to grow.

The Purpose This is a fantastic debrief question. Go to that curious place you're developing as a leader and just wonder, *"What happened?"* If something didn't work, *"What happened?"* When a plan failed, *"What happened?"*

Curiosity is oxygen to the leader looking to grow. Be genuinely curious. Be gentle on yourself. Simply ask, *"What happened?"* Then dig. Journal it out. I cannot emphasize strongly enough the power of journaling. When we write out our story, we see connections that were hidden, and can draw conclusions we didn't realize were there. Thinking about it is good, but it won't get to the heart of the issue.

Was there a mistake you made? Were there things out of your control? Seek to understand where things went awry. If the other person says they were lazy or just didn't get to it, that helps frame the next questions and reset expectations. If there was something hidden from the leader's view or a complicating factor the person identifies, then the conversation can go with those facts and truths.

Ask this question of your people. Rather than, *"Why did you do that?"* go to a place of curiosity with, *"What happened?"* Leaders who will be curious with their people will develop curiosity in their people.

Level Up your Leadership with this Question for Today.

QUESTION 16 | The Story

More clients than I can count fall into this leadership trap. Rather than an attitude of curiosity when something goes wrong, or not according to plan, many leaders go immediately to, *"What did you do wrong?"* or *"Why did you do it that way?"* or *"Let me in there!"*

There tend to be two common data points:

1. The view of failure

2. The positive feeling from fixing

When viewed as a personal statement on them, failure can derail leadership. All this leader sees is how others will view themselves if a project fails. Better to do it themselves rather than risk failure by delegating it to others.

Then there is *"The Fixer."* This person gets a fix from fixing situations and people. This leader, like the one above, makes it about themselves rather than the situation. It could be a matter of trusting people that needs to grow. Maybe it's control.

Both of these leaders do not learn from failure, the best teacher we have. They believe that failure is final or is personal. But it's not. New self-talk, a reframing of failure, and not owning what is not yours are some of the stepping stones I have used to walk alongside clients to help level up their leadership.

What keeps you from this question?

QUESTION 16 | The Application

1. Develop curiosity as your go-to mindset. Find a question mark to put on your desk, stick on your phone, post on your computer screen, hang in your car, etc.

2. Is there a failure, recent or not, that haunts your mind? Journal it out with an attitude of curiosity. See what you discover. Keep a productive attitude.

QUESTION 17 | Do I see people or problems?

Leadership is first about relationships.

The Purpose Are people a necessary bother to you? Are they unpredictable, unreliable, untrustworthy? Or are people human beings with emotions and connections? Do they feel deeply and passionately? Do they want to grow and learn?

Leaders who answer this question with people versus problems will lead differently.

Human beings are emotional, filled with dreams and passions, scarred by hurts and tragedies. Some are insecure while others are over-confident. If you approach people as problems, you will not trust your team. You will tend to micro-manage, having your radar up for any slacking off that might occur. Because people can't be trusted, they are a problem.

Problems have to be micro-managed and watched. You have to check up on problems, even gathering evidence for your pre-conclusion that they are trying to get away with something. You can't let them. That's a lot of pressure that leads to stress.

However, if you see people, you will tend to lead through connection. You will take time to chit-chat, seeing the activity as an essential piece of leading people rather than a waste of time. The care you express to others will build relationships, and that's what people need.

Level Up your Leadership with this Question for Today.

QUESTION 17 | The Story

During my 30 years as a Pastor, friends and colleagues would often ask, *"How's the Church going?"* I enjoyed responding, "Great, if it weren't for the people!"

Any time you get more than one human being in a room, there is going to be disagreement and potential conflict. But does that mean the people are the problem?

Joe saw people as problems. He believed they had to be driven, that you had to be tough on them. Otherwise they wouldn't do what was necessary for the team to succeed. He would lay out the processes for the team to follow and expected others to follow the plan exactly. When someone didn't, Joe pointed it out and took over. There was one way and it was Joe's way. Joe could train but he couldn't let go. People couldn't be trusted.

Joe was good at what he did. He was exact and precise. When Joe was around, the other leaders were at ease. Should anything go wrong, Joe could make it work. But Joe's team was timid and fearful around him.

Nothing was ever good enough, so people dropped off the teams. Pretty soon it was the whole organization that adjusted, even abandoning some of their ideas – all to avoid conflicts with Joe. In reality, Joe was the one who was most afraid. It was a hard truth. Joe was afraid that people would abandon him, not stick with him for a long-term relationship. His harsh words and pointing finger created a buffer zone into which no one was allowed. It was a way to protect himself that worked, until it didn't.

Slowly we broke through. Self-acceptance was first and then he learned to ask better questions to find out more information. He began to inquire about the lives of the people on his team. Relationships grew and hope replaced despair. He saw people as people.

QUESTION 17 | The Application

1. When you go on vacation, leaving your connected world for some downtime, what do you worry about? Do you check remote cameras back at work? Do you check in with people to make sure they are doing this or that? Or do you disconnect and let your people lead?

2. Find some ways to celebrate your people just because they are people. For instance, if you have a small team, go around and tell everyone you're headed to a coffee shop and you're buying. Hand out gift cards for birthdays or a job well done. Write a name on a white board in the organization, recognizing someone who went above and beyond that week.

JESTION 18 | **Where can I simplify my life?**

mplicity provides freedom and energy.

ie Purpose A complicated life, where the calendar is filled, allows no time for self-care, which is not a good foundation upon which to build leadership success. Simplicity provides freedom and energy. If you spend all your money before the paycheck arrives, it creates stress and anxiety, with no margin for surprise delays and detours.

Where can I simply my life? is a reality check on being human. Where are you practicing a regular rhythm of rest, knowing that going, going, and going isn't healthy in the long run? How are you prioritizing the most important relationships in your life, with family and close friends?

Where can you downsize rather than increase? What can you strip away and do without? Can you go another year or generation without the latest technological update?

You may know the *Pareto Principle*, from the Italian economist. 80 percent of what you do brings 20 percent of the results. 20 percent of what you do brings 80 percent of the results. Simplicity is a companion behavior to this 80-20 principle.

Take an inventory of your calendar, your budget, your relationships, and your work. I have a tool I use that helps clients discover areas of imbalance so they can choose more accurately where to focus on change. If you'd like to receive it, send me an email at Jeff@levelupleadershipcoach.com, and ask for the *"Life Wheel."*

Level Up your Leadership with this Question for Today.

QUESTION 18 | The Story

John said to me, *"But I just can't be gone."*

He was referring to taking time off, using his vacation, and releasing things to his staff team. Some might call him controlling, and I wouldn't argue with it. He certainly enjoys getting into the fray and mixing it up, looking at all angles and arguing counterpoints just to make sure they get to the bottom of the issue at hand.

Not knowing was hard for him. He also liked being in control.

Through our coaching engagement we worked on what that 20 percent was in his role that would bring 80 percent of his results. It was not an easy journey. Too much could go wrong. Too many things could happen and he needed to be there to save the day. The truth was he enjoyed fixing things, situations, and people. The realization was he made those things, situations, and other people's problems all about himself.

John learned that leaving his staff alone to deal with whatever came along was one way to grow their leadership. As his staff grew, John was able to focus more on the things that only John could do. This was his 20 percent.

He was emotional, sometimes laughing and sometimes running frazzled from here to there, with no time for the very people he was seeking to inspire. Simplification for John was delegating and releasing. He had an underlying issue that if his people failed, the world would end. It was fear about the impact of the failure.

Simplifying your life is a wide doorway into better leadership.

QUESTION 18 | The Application

1. Do you have an idea of what your 20 percent is? Be aware that it exists and begin whittling it down. Perhaps start with a list that may number ten to twelve things.

2. What is the real issue for you: delegation, trust, fear of missing out (FOMO), wanting to be enough, being a fixer? Be honest about it. Lay it out there so you can deal with it.

3. What other issues could have been going on in John's life that led to similar behaviors and attitudes? Do you see the possibilities in yourself?

JESTION 19 | **How did I cause this?**

ccountability begins with the leader.

he Purpose This is a hard question, but a necessary one, to level up your leadership.

The successful leader looks first to herself, asking where she may have missed a step or not communicated clearly enough when a project doesn't go well. Accountability begins with the leader, the captain on the bridge, before looking at others.

Was your communication unclear in some way? Did you take into account to whom you were talking? Was there a conflict you were avoiding, perhaps not holding someone accountable? Did you not have a process for accountability that wasn't personal but focused on the issue at hand? As you can see, the questions are endless, but must be asked.

Figuring out your role in how things went wrong is part of the learning curve. The leader who starts blaming others or the circumstances around herself will not grow and will continue to make the same mistakes. If the team fails, the leader takes responsibility. If the team succeeds, the leader shares the credit.

Level Up your Leadership with this Question for Today.

QUESTION 19 | The Story

One of my staff members resigned, but only after throwing a fit. My board reinstated her and told me to deal with it. My Church Administrator, Dan, and I were bewildered. Now what?

So we met with my leadership coach, in the coffee shop we could see from our building. We strode confidently to the corner table. Explaining the situation, we anticipated a question. We didn't have to wait long. It wasn't a very good question by coaching standards: "You realize you caused this, don't you?" She gave us the answer in the question. Painful. Also true.

We dissected where we had gone wrong. My experience in coaching others has shown the common pitfalls into which we fell.

We abandoned responsibility because we didn't agree with the decision. We didn't get into a room with the staff member and ourselves to think through this together. Instead, we avoided it. Not helpful.

We had an opportunity to find out more information, to communicate more clearly, and to set all of us up for success. In the end, it wasn't about us. It was about the mission of the organization. But we made it about us.

About a month later the staff person resigned again, with an apology to both of us. She owned her behavior as not acceptable and understood it. We had to own our behavior as not acceptable and lead differently into the future.

QUESTION 19 | The Application

1. What do you avoid in leadership? Conflict? Deeper relationships?

2. Do you have a conversation you *"need"* to have, one you are avoiding? Consider writing out what you need to say. Perfect it. Make an appointment and take your note with you. Read it so that you won't say too much and you won't leave anything out.

QUESTION 20 | Am I striving for a work-life balance that doesn't exist?

The work-life balance is a myth. It's more about choosing where to cheat.

The Purpose The work-life balance is a myth. It doesn't exist. There will always be choices to make.

I challenge leaders with this question to help them focus on things that are beyond temporary. For some it's a spiritual eternity. For others it's factual, that they don't want to achieve great business success and find they have no one with which to share it in the end.

In some ways it's called *"choosing to cheat."* That's such an emotionally laden word, but stay with me. Work will take all the time you are willing to give it, and without much awareness of the time involved. Work is always waiting and is always there. Family is always waiting, too, and will take as much time as you give them. You're either going to cheat work or cheat your family. You get to choose.

As in the movie *Indiana Jones and the Last Crusade*, the old Knight says, *"You must choose ... but choose wisely. For as the true grail will bring you life, the false grail will take it from you."* There is a lot of truth in there for the choice we must make about where we will cheat.

Think of it this way: If work is an idol, then rest will feel like a sin. That's not balance. It's more about choices. All the riches in the world mean nothing if there aren't people with whom we can share them. My friend, Mark, gave me a great approach: *"I strive for work-life harmony. It's much less stressful."*

Level Up your Leadership with this Question for Today.

QUESTION 20 | The Story

Meeting with a church leadership team for the first time, I was asked, *"What's your usual schedule like?"* I answered, *"I will put in the 80-hour weeks when necessary and I won't apologize for the 35-hour weeks when they come."* That was how I sought to strike some kind of balance.

I sought to limit my nights away, to organize the church administration in ways that didn't require me to be there at all times. I sought to develop leaders to whom I could delegate leadership. I chose to make my kids' sports competitions and participate in driving to practices. I chose to make Sunday worship a priority – oh, wait, that was part of my job!

I took all of my vacation. I took my day off each week. And I didn't apologize for it. Did the churches I led grow as big or as fast as they could have, had I sacrificed more family time? Perhaps not. And perhaps they wouldn't have anyway. Every time I got back from being gone, work was still there.

This choice did mean that I worked after the kids were in bed. I found a way to do some desk or computer work while they were at sports practices. I did have the advantage to adjust my schedule like that. But people didn't check with me about a crisis they had or about a death. That's where you adjust and meet the need that exists.

What does that look like in your job? I've watched people work themselves silly, gain much recognition and riches, and lose their families. I chose what I thought was most worthwhile and that's what finding balance is all about. I'm not suggesting I did it perfectly and you won't either. But I did have a plan and so can you.

QUESTION 20 | The Application

1. Are you taking all of your vacation? If not, begin to block it out now. Schedule it before it gets scheduled away.

2. When can you block out times in your calendar for family and friends? What times of the day? Times of the week? Times each month?

3. Are you working so much because you have a lot of debts to pay? Consider getting with a financial coach. Trim back your expenses. Sometimes we end up serving our stuff rather than our stuff being a tool to help us enjoy one another. By the way, I happen to be a Dave Ramsey Master Financial Coach. Let me know how I can be helpful.

QUESTION 21 | **When am I at my best?**

Prioritizing yourself is not selfish. It's about being at your best for those you lead and serve.

The Purpose

Are you a morning person or more of an evening one? Do you focus better at one time or another? One part of the week over another? Each individual human being has a rhythm that works for them. Do you know yours?

So much of life drains energy from you. What do you do to replenish yourself? It's a self-care question but goes deeper. What are the behaviors that fill you up?

What are the activities that you find to be life giving? What relationships need to be healthy for you to be able to focus and be at your best? I think it is not too far a stretch to say that if home isn't clicking, then work won't be clicking. These are relationships that give us life or they completely drain energy from us.

Are you an introvert or an extrovert? Do you gain energy from solitude or from being around others? If you work better when you have more alone time, then schedule it. Do you thrive more when you are around people? Make sure you are around people. Successful leaders don't apologize for who they are and what they need. They know. And they behave in ways that leverage the strengths of who they are.

Each human being has value to add to others.

Level Up your Leadership with this Question for Today.

QUESTION 21 | The Story

This is one of my favorite questions. It's in the self-care category, a place that we often don't like to go. Maybe we believe we don't have time for it. It's a key leadership question that helps me focus. In my 30s I came across a similar question and it sent me on a quest to figure out what had to be happening in my life to bring me energy and focus. I discovered that I could deliberately pursue some activities and a pace of life that would help me. These activities do not need to be every day, but they need to be a consistent part of my life.

In fact, when I find myself highly stressed or anxious, I can look at my list and I guarantee you that one or more of these pieces has been consistently missing.

It takes some experimentation and requires a high level of self-awareness. It will take some time. It's worth the journey.

I settled on the following list:

1. Dating my wife. The most important relationship has to be right.

2. Spiritual and physical exercise.

3. Grandparent time. My grandchildren bring me life

4. Teaching, coaching, mentoring. My sweet spot is working with people.

5. The world of swimming. My sport of choice as a competitor and official.

What is on your list? Give it time and you will be richly rewarded.

QUESTION 21 | The Application

1. Make your list of 5 things. You might start with 7 or 8 or 10, but whittle it down to a manageable 5. This took me a year to perfect, tweaking it here and there. So take your time with it.

2. Write time in your calendar for yourself, with something you already know is on your list of 5. Do it now before your time gets scheduled away.

QUESTION 22 | What are the first words out of my mouth?

The words we speak first determine the direction we will move.

The Purpose First words and thoughts often betray our deep-seated feelings and even our comfort zone. Where do we run when we hear a new idea? Some people welcome new ideas and tend to speak positive words or perhaps no words at all (which doesn't necessarily mean they agree). Others don't like an idea unless they came up with it! And still others speak negatively with their first words because they don't know how it will work, and they must know how it will work.

Who are you? What are your first words? What do your first words communicate to those who hear your words?

Everyone can improve from where they are, but do you highlight only the negative? Where do you go first with your focus? Negativity won't get you very far. It will breed frustration in your people. Positivity, on the other hand, creates momentum and will breed success.

Our own frustration will lead to negative words. As a leader, choose to look inward for the answer to why, before blaming others. What leads your words?

It's okay to ask for time to think. It's great leadership to ask for more information. A result of negative words being your first words is that people will stop bringing you new ideas. You will decrease creativity in your team or company.

Level Up your Leadership with this Question for Today.

QUESTION 22 | The Story

"No."

Literally, this is often the first word from her mouth. If it isn't the first, it is the second. Then it's off to the races, which only ends in frustration and arguments and nowhere good. That's why I was brought in, to coach this brilliant, hard-working leader who wasn't going anywhere if she didn't, well, get over herself and her need to be right. More than that, to prove how right she was to everyone she met.

If you were on the other end of her pointing finger, it communicated everything negative you could imagine. She had brilliant ideas, and, probably more often than not, she was right. Our work was hard, trudging slowly out of this pit she had dug until there came a time for this image: Who is going to be sharing your victories with you in the end?

She sat silent. That's when I know I've hit on or very close to the bullseye with a client. A driven leader, who pushes others away with their quick words and negativity, finally realizes where that behavior ends. She could choose to be right and let everyone know it. Or she could choose to focus on building right relationships, even with people who had different views.

We were able to craft a new behavior that asked questions first, seeking more information. Through this new behavior my client communicated to the other person that she was listening. Many times, because her brilliance hadn't changed, things still ended up in a place where she was correct. Now other people were standing with her rather than on the other side of the line she had drawn.

Better relationships led to better productivity, greater employee engagement, and a more pleasant atmosphere where people wanted to work together.

QUESTION 22 | The Application

1. Pay attention to your words today. What is your tendency and what are the circumstances around them?

2. Make a list of positive words or questions you can ask rather than going negative. These might include: Could you tell me more about it?

3. Take note of your body language. If your words change from negative to positive but you still cross your arms, frown, or use a condescending tone, the impact will be the same.

QUESTION 23 | Do I need to forgive?

Forgiveness: I give up my right to hurt you for hurting me.

The Purpose

Forgiveness is a most powerful leadership behavior. Forgiveness is an essential part of every healthy relationship. It's the key to relationships.

Do you wake up thinking about someone with whom you have a conflict?

Do you find yourself praying for a person and end up having a conversation with that person, even though they are not present? These are indications that you may be harboring some unforgiveness in your heart.

Forgiveness is a choice, a decision that we make. It is not a feeling. Regardless of the attitude or actions of the other person, to lead well means to take the initiative in this drama.

Forgiveness means that you give up your right to hurt others who have hurt you. It's truthful about the hurt, which is a vital step in the right direction.

You don't have to be best friends. Reconciliation is a two-way street. Forgiveness is a decision that can be made by one. By you.

Ask yourself this question when you find your heart unsettled, or you feel stuck and uncertain about what to do next. Holding onto unforgiveness means that hurt will be leading your life rather you leading yourself by choice. Your decision will impact your people whichever way you choose.

Level Up your Leadership with this Question for Today.

QUESTION 23 | The Story

As a leader, having thick skin and being quick to forgive are essential qualities.

A seminary professor said, *"You cannot hold unforgiveness in your heart any more than you can ingest broken glass into your physical body. They will both tear you up from the inside out."*

After 25 years of leading Churches, I was unceremoniously shown the door by a church board. It was both ugly and difficult, with accusations and assumptions, as well as the truth of some poor leadership choices from me.

It was emotionally difficult. I wanted to lead with my forgiveness foot. At the meeting where their decision was announced, I said, *"Whatever happens, I hold no grudge against you."* It was a step in the right direction. But the feelings persisted.

Months later I was able to take advantage of a spiritual retreat offer with my alma mater, Asbury Theological Seminary. Part of the offering was to meet with a spiritual director. During that meeting, he said: "It sounds like you are holding some unforgiveness."

"What?" I thought to myself. *"No way. I forgave them from day one."* The months separating the board meeting and this spiritual director meeting should have been enough, so I thought. It was time to decide once again to walk in forgiveness.

After three years of walking this pathway, making myself accountable to a few others, and giving myself permission to not always be okay, slowly feelings caught up with the decision. That's the pathway of forgiveness. This was how I chose to lead myself rather than be led by unforgiveness.

In this way I was able to lead myself rather than being led by a tightly held unforgiveness.

QUESTION 23 | The Story

1. What are the hurts and grudges that you are holding against others? Make a list and make a choice to forgive. This may be a lengthy process. Just go one step at a time. You might choose to write them a letter expressing what you'd like to say. You're not sending the letter, just writing it out.

2. Make a choice to not hold grudges from this day forward. Make a motion with your hands: hold them tightly in front of you to symbolize a grudge, then loosen your grip like anticipating a hug to symbolize forgiveness.

3. Ask for help from someone you trust will be understanding but firm with you. There's no shame in needing help with this deeply emotional process.

QUESTION 24 | What is my evidence for this conclusion?

Assumptions are the Achilles heel of a leader.

The Purpose Assumptions are a foundational leadership mistake. Stop yourself and ask, What is my evidence for this conclusion?

A different way to ask it is, Do I have all the information I need to make an informed decision? Or, Am I making this decision based on evidence or my own feelings?

Leaders who jump to conclusions will find themselves spending time walking back statements and mandates. It comes naturally to some who just want to get things done, like making cuts that look right. The woodworker who measures twice before cutting once, will be more precise, ruin less boards, and pieces meant to fit together will actually fit.

Take a moment to draw your conclusions. Is that person really being mean? Is that person really brain dead? Check your evidence. Asking this question will help your leadership step forward on a solid footing.

Be careful on the other side of this question as well. If you are sensitive, compassionate, and caring, you may have a tendency to own other people's feelings, causing you to draw conclusions without evidence. Thoughts and feelings are just thoughts and feelings. They are not right or wrong. The behaviors that proceed from them are where you focus as a leader.

Level Up your Leadership with this Question for Today.

QUESTION 24 | The Story

Emotional leaders will tend to draw conclusions quickly, based on how they feel: perhaps angry, frustrated, or tired. But also, there are people who are hyper-sensitive about how others feel, and they will draw conclusions based on their own feelings from the other side. These overly sensitive people will own other people's feelings and often believe they are responsible for healing those feelings.

A client who has a tremendous heart for people knows this about himself. Mike is a guy you can trust, knowing he will keep a confidence and will listen to you as if you are the only person in the world at that moment. When faced with a conflict, especially in a group setting, he will focus on how to fix the feelings of everyone in the group rather than focus on the issue at hand. This leads to drawing conclusions without evidence.

Mike also knows how other people will feel and how they will think. He draws conclusions based on his ownership of others' feelings. I asked him one time if he wore a t-shirt with a large "S" on it because he sure had x-ray vision into people's souls. He laughed a painful, knowing laugh.

No matter which side of this question you tend toward, stop yourself from drawing conclusions without evidence. If you're like Mike, know that you are not responsible for healing the feelings of others. If you are a more reactive leader, who spurts out conclusions without thinking, understand it is not helpful to your leadership. Find a way to stop yourself. Get a coach!

Let the evidence guide you rather than your assumptions. The two will sometimes coincide, but not always.

QUESTION 24 | The Application

1. Do you notice a tendency in your assumptions? Do you assume more with certain people or particular situations? Pay attention and ask yourself what triggers are at work there.

2. Carry a list of three or four questions to memorize and then pair it with a reminder: a tchotchke, a steampunk coin, a smooth rock, etc. Carry them both in your pocket to remind you to ask questions before sharing your wealth of knowledge. Options might include:

   - Can you tell me more?
   - Because?
   - And?

QUESTION 25 | **What is stopping me?**

To avoid, delay, deflect, or blame is not leadership.

The Purpose When you notice a hesitation, ask yourself this question: What is stopping me?

When you become aware that you know what you need to do but can't bring yourself to do it, ask yourself: What is stopping me?

Avoidance behaviors such as delay, procrastination, deflection, and blame, all work to feed something in you. Perhaps it's a conversation you need to have with a colleague or subordinate, and because you assume it will cause conflict, your assumption stops you. Some don't want to bother with what they consider a waste of time, the idle chit-chat that develops relationships. Because they are so driven toward their goals, even people are a distraction and bother. Is that what is stopping you? What do you fear about it?

There are people who won't do or try anything that they aren't sure they know how to do. What's that about? Avoidance behaviors help us avoid pain: emotional, physical, mental. They also help us avoid success. An elite athlete has to have the mentality that pain is just a part of the process. That's a big reason why there are very few Olympians in the world. The anticipation of pain stops many athletes from their peak performance.

Be honest with yourself.

Level Up your Leadership with this Question for Today.

QUESTION 25 | The Story

Tom is my friend, mentor, and colleague in coaching. He is also the author of the Foreword to this book. Tom said to me, with a wave of his hand: "Okay. All the barriers are gone now. What will you do?"

From his home in London, England he reached through the Zoom screen to my office in Cincinnati, Ohio. I was getting ready to make the leap to full-time executive leadership coaching and found a hesitation. I knew some of what I needed to do, mainly around marketing. Was fear stopping me? Probably, at least in part. Was uncertainty stopping me? It was probably also playing a role.

"All the barriers are gone now. What will you do?" asked Tom. It was a brilliant coaching moment from Tom and a learning moment for me. It freed me to see clearly my next step.

I look at this as a key moment to opening the next doors to my business. It is a simple trick that can help you get unstuck. Everyone needs tricks to assist, remind, and motivate. Don't be afraid of them or think you shouldn't need them.

When I first started doing my *"1-Minute Question for Today"* videos, I was terrified. Would people like them? Would social media castigate me? Would anyone watch? I had to remember what I coach people to remember: confident feelings always follow confident actions. I had to get honest with what was stopping me so that I could forge ahead. One way I did that was to send the first video to a small group of trusted friends whom I knew would be honest and gentle with their feedback.

What is stopping me? will give you pause. Ask it of a direct report, What is stopping you? You will help them think it through. That's what a coach does.

QUESTION 25 | The Application

1. Pretend the barriers stopping you are gone. What would you do? Wave a pretend magic wand in front of a mirror and tell yourself that the barriers are gone. Now what?

2. What is a project that is stalled right now? Name one step toward that goal, i.e., send a video to a friend for feedback. Do that one step.

QUESTION 26 | What is my relationship to conflict?

Conflict is inevitable. Conflict without casualties is leadership.

The Purpose Leadership is defined by how you handle conflict. Conflict is inevitable when more than one human being is present in the same place. In fact, conflict may be present even with just one person.

This question goes to the heart of the issue. It's not as much about do you avoid conflict or create conflict (yes, there are some people who thrive in conflict), but rather what is your relationship to conflict? If conflict is seen as negative at all times, this will lead to lack of leadership when conflict is needed. If, on the other hand, conflict is your comfort zone, then you will tend to create conflict when it isn't needed.

What is conflict to you? Can you disagree agreeably? When you need to hold a direct report accountable for an expectation you set, is it a negative in your mind? Is every disagreement defined as conflict to you?

Can you see ways that conflict can be constructive? Where every point of contention doesn't have to end in a casualty of the relationship?

How you define conflict will determine your pathway through the maze of human relationships. This is leadership.

Level Up your Leadership with this Question for Today.

QUESTION 26 | The Story

Patrick is one of my favorite clients. We've met him before in this book. He is passionate, hard-working, intelligent, and he genuinely cares about people. His biggest deficit, however, is when his passion about reaching his goal overtakes his care and concern for his people. Patrick loves to get into the fray with his staff and their people. For him, what others see as conflict is his comfort zone.

But this doesn't work for everyone, and it took a long time for Patrick to realize it. He loved to mix it up, challenging people's thoughts – almost like engaging on the martial arts mats at his gym. What this did to his people was communicate that he didn't care and wasn't listening.

He challenged me, which was not a surprise, that the issue wasn't his lack of listening but rather when his actions didn't follow the other person's thoughts. That other person would say he didn't listen.

We were able to discover a way around this by making sure he asked the right questions, took time to pause, and looked like he was listening. It's amazing that when we put our bodies in a listening posture, we actually listen better. His responses became person centered rather than goal centered and everyone's goals were more consistently reached.

The impact? People trusted him more and the whole team was more effective at reaching their goals. It's a work in progress, as it is for all leaders. It's people who reach goals, but it has to be people first for the leader.

QUESTION 26 The Application

1. Write down a definition of conflict before turning to the dictionary to compare and contrast. What's the difference?

2. What IS your relationship with conflict? Always negative? What has to happen for conflict to be positive?

3. Consider a present, conflicted relationship at work. Write out a win-win scenario and then see how you can pursue it one step at a time.

QUESTION 27 | What is your desired outcome?

Are you trying to win or are you seeking to develop people?

The Purpose Like many of our questions, this one can be self-coaching or one for you to ask of others. Asking about the desired outcome can help you reach your goals. The question can also come alongside you as you manage the relationships of work.

On the self-coaching side, asking about the desired outcome will help bring clarity to your next steps. The old adage that if you don't know where you are heading, any old route will do, rings true. Asking yourself this question will help you focus on what is important. What is it you are really after? And is your present behavior helping get you there?

Are you trying to win or are you seeking to develop people? Those are two different results that come from different behaviors.

When posing this question to others it will help them focus. It's a great question to ask those difficult people in your life. The person who argues every point, or who stirs up conflict at every turn, can be stopped in their tracks with this question. They will either come up with an answer or they won't have an answer – and that will be an answer.

Rather than random actions and words, ask yourself and others about desired outcomes. It will help everyone become clear about the steps to take.

Level Up your Leadership with this Question for Today.

QUESTION 27 | The Story

He pushed and pushed and pushed, like a dog that wouldn't drop a bone. He would text single questions to me, to others, and sometimes a small group of us. We all wondered aloud: *"What is he driving at?"* We wanted him to just say it. We wanted him to be up front. It felt subversive, as if he had an agenda.

"What's your desired outcome with this line of questions?" I asked.

He was taken aback and silent. I asked it a different way: *"What are you hoping to accomplish?"*

He admitted that he was seeking to prove his assumptions by gathering information. He wanted his way because he was convinced, at all times, that his way was the best way. It was also his way of avoiding the appearance that he didn't know. He equated not knowing with failure, and it was personal. That's quite a leap when you stand back and look at it but not unusual in many people.

With difficult people, I have posed this question and received two basic responses:

1) pausing to ponder, and authentically wonder to themselves what the point is;

2) defensiveness and deflecting to argue about what they assume is behind the question. Crazy-makers will always be crazy-makers. It is just not worth engaging with them, and that is sad for me to write. I value people. I don't value the crazy-making.

Whether you ask this question to bring clarity to your next steps or to come alongside a crazy-making, difficult person, let the question sit there in silence while it is pondered.

QUESTION 27 | The Application

1. Early in my life I was encouraged to aim for four things in every Sunday message. How do you do at these in your life?

- Making people laugh
- Making people cry
- Making people think
- Giving people a question that keeps them up at night

2. What is your desired outcome with people? business? family? There can be a major difference between winning and building healthy relationships. Which are you after?

QUESTION 28 | # Which do I believe first: the best or the worst?

Believe the best and your people will give you their best.

The Purpose

Positivity helps leaders lead more effectively. I've seen it work in my coaching. I've seen it work in leading people. When leaders believe in their people, their people believe more in themselves than they could alone.

When something goes wrong on your team or in your company, what is your first belief? The clue may be in the question you tend to ask first. Is it, What did you do wrong? Or is it, What happened? The accusatory and negative question will deflate your people. Avoid this as a first question.

When a team member comes to you sharing a frustration or a roadblock they are up against, do you believe the best or the worst? Is your default viewpoint that the person has done something wrong?

If you believe your people are capable and competent, this approach will lead to greater trust. You will grow confidence in your people. They'll lead better. You'll lead better. It could be that something dumb happened, not caused by anyone. Believe the best and your people will give you their best.

Level Up your Leadership with this Question for Today.

QUESTION 28 | The Story

"What did you do wrong?" When she realized this was often the first thing out of her mouth she was astonished and embarrassed. The coaching relationship is like holding up a mirror to a client so they can see what they really do. Often it's shocking. Sometimes a client knows what they do and even that it's not helpful, but they don't know what to do about it. This is where we ended up.

Sarah is a brilliant leader. Strong. Bright. She will tackle any mountain, hill, or valley between her and her goal. She's also fun. She smiles and doesn't let surprises detour her. It's an interesting combination of determination and the awareness of what really matters. But what sets her off more than anything else is when her people make silly, costly mistakes.

This tendency to go to the negative side when confronting a mistake led to unintended consequences. She instilled fear in her people, which may have actually led to more mistakes. The shift came in how Sarah viewed the situation and a new behavior she installed in her life through our coaching.

She began to start from a place of curiosity as well as the assumption that something went wrong that was out of anyone's control. The problem would certainly be fixed, but because her people received support and positivity first, they actually got better at their jobs. Fear is a poor motivator in the long run. This change in leadership was proof.

QUESTION 28 | The Application

1. Do you believe everyone has potential to grow and learn? Do you believe you have potential to grow and learn?

2. What do you believe about people? Are they cheaters, lazy, and have to be pushed and watched over, or do you believe they are hard-working, helpful, and desire to meet expectations? Consider the different paths depending on your starting place. How does each impact your words? Your actions? Your attitude?

QUESTION 29 | Do I use too many words? Or not enough?

Carefully chosen words will create clear communication.

The Purpose Words are important. How many do you use? Some people use too many and others use too few. When the amount of words is too many, it clouds your communication. Your people will not know which words they should listen to. Some of your people will check out and not hear most of what you say. Do you know who they are? If you tend to ramble, telling people how to build a watch when they asked you what time it was, you will be perceived as incompetent.

On the other hand, if you don't use enough words, your people will have to fill in the blanks for themselves. If you only say, *"Just get it done,"* they will do it in whatever way they wish. It may not be what you want. Clear explanations and expectations build fully functioning teams. Some leaders process their thoughts out loud. You must be very careful if this is you. Alert people to what you are doing while reducing how often you do it. Many of the people you lead listen to what you say and want to do a job well. But the mess of words confuses them.

Other leaders process internally and only after careful thought do they speak words out loud. This can create a slow process for making decisions and there is a chance some of your people will walk ahead of you because they are tired of waiting. Let people know where you are in your process.

Carefully chosen words will create clear communication.

Level Up your Leadership with this Question for Today.

QUESTION 29 | The Story

Ray spoke first and thought second. This is not a helpful way to communicate. What we uncovered in our coaching sessions was that his words were a way to push people away. If people really engaged with him, Ray thought, and really got to know him, they wouldn't like him. These people would not stick with him for the long haul, so it was easier to erect some walls with words.

The impact on the people he interacted with was detrimental to both relationships and production. Ray didn't see it at first. He insisted that people do things his way, and more often than not, his way did work. But it was dictatorial not collaborative. The approach kept people at a distance.

This habit also resulted in conflict. Ray was a master at stirring up conflict. Again, conflict was another way to keep people at bay, deflecting the conversation away from things that might cause introspection and lead to healthy relationships. This was Ray's comfort zone and while it was horrible, it was comfortable. He knew how to behave in it. He knew what to expect.

As is often the case with clients, getting Ray to pause and ask an open-ended question was a big part of our work. He began to see people not as a problem to be managed but as humans with emotions, feelings, and opinions. This was a hard road, breaking through the fear zone, and finding freedom in back-and-forth conversation without demeaning the other person. People wanted to actually be on Ray's team when they experienced his change.

Ray was already a master at training people. He became a better delegator. He also became a trusted friend to many.

QUESTION 29 | The Application

1. Pay attention to your words. How many do you use? Do you answer the question asked or do you give more information than is necessary?

2. Try an experiment with your words: before you answer a question, say, *"Give me a second to think about that."* This will give you time to consider carefully the words you end up saying.

3. If you are a verbal processor, speaking what you are thinking and therefore saying too many words, try this experiment: Tell people you are thinking out loud for a moment. Then tell them when you are ready for your conclusion.

QUESTION 30 | **What are the 3 things that only I can do?**

The 3 Things are the Compass rather than the Calendar. They are the hidden things that support the visible things.

The Purpose This is a great question to wrap up this first book of leadership questions. It can be the launching pad for what's next, unlocking potential and impact. There are 3 Things that you do which no one else can do. What are they? People push back, *"I have 100 things to do!"*

3 Things. Seriously. What are they for you? When you discover these 3 Things, you will experience the power of keystone habits. These are actions that unlock other things automatically.

A simple illustration. If I begin a consistent exercise routine, my eating habits, sleeping habits, and energy levels will automatically be impacted. They will change, perhaps along with my clothes size too. Your 3 Things work the same way.

Your 3 Things are those key activities that only you can do. If you don't do them, they won't get done, because the people on your team have other things to do.

Your 3 Things lie in Stephen Covey's, Quadrant 2: the important but not urgent. (4) The 3 Things are the Compass rather than the Calendar. They are the hidden things that support the visible things.

Level Up your Leadership with this Question for Today.

QUESTION 30 | The Story

My client could not see clearly how to dwindle his long list of jobs down to 3 Things. He is the CEO of his small company and in order to grow to the next level, he needed to lead differently. He just didn't know how. So we started this project.

Once Aaron got there, the floodgates opened to the possibilities. Because I had taught him a process for setting clear expectations and holding people accountable, he was able to delegate with confidence in strategic ways. What was the result?

His company grew during an economic time when others of similar size and industry were not growing. As Aaron owned his 3 Things and stuck to them, his people gained confidence and took more pride in their work. It was like the boss had handed them a share of the company's future. Aaron began concentrating his energy and focus on the business rather than in the business.

In some ways, moving to his 3 Things was like moving from the role of a shepherd to that of a rancher. No longer did Aaron interact with some of the people in the company and all of their clients. Now his main time was spent with the people who connected with those people. Not everyone can make that transition. It's not a right or wrong, good or bad thing either way. But to scale the company, it is a move Aaron needed to make.

QUESTION 30 | The Application

1. Would you like to start your list? Are you ready to let go of some things?

2. Send me an email (Jeff@levelupleadershipcoach.com) and let's get together to whittle down your list to those 3 Things that will Level Up your leadership. Because you have purchased this book, I will discount this first session to $50. We'll spend an hour together and then you can decide if you want to continue.